FAMILIAR IMAGES

© 2018 Ellen Moore Osborne
www.TrinityArts.com
Ellen@TrinityArts.com

This is a verbatim reproduction of the author's
1991 thesis statement and artwork,
under the name Ellen E. Moore.
The addendum features photographs from the show.
All rights reserved.

ISBN-13: 978-1983642432
ISBN-10: 1983642436

Cover image:
House of Viar • 1990 • Mixed Media Collage • 28" x 38"

FAMILIAR IMAGES

A Thesis

Submitted to the Graduate Faculty of the
Louisiana State University and
Agricultural and Mechanical College
in partial fulfillment of the
requirements for the degree of
Master of Fine Arts

in

The School of Art

By
Ellen E. Moore
B.F.A., East Carolina University, 1986
May 1991

ACKNOWLEDGEMENT

I would like to thank my Baton Rouge family: Kellee Walters, Boo Radley, Elizabeth "Squeak" MaGillicuddy, and Popeye, for their constant encouragement and entertainment.

ABSTRACT

This body of work is a series of intaglios and collages dealing with the plausibility of combining photographically derived images with traditional forms of mark-making. The subject matter involves the tradition of family photographs and the history of photographic printmaking.

LIST OF ILLUSTRATIONS

Buster and the Cat 2
Wait—Don't Go. 4
Portrait of My Uncle as a Cowboy 6
In Remembrance of the Porch Photos 8
Deluxe American Kitty Hostage 10
Ideal Street Teepees 12

FAMILIAR IMAGES

The body of work I refer to as "Familiar Images" deals directly with the technical possibilities of combining drawing marks made by hand and images delineated by light during a photographic process. These works are the result of searching for the right combination of ways to alter and add to photographic images in their printed form. I have found the indirectness of the intaglio medium causes it to be the most conducive means of presenting photographic images and hand created images in the same format. The printed intaglio shows no definition of the ways the separate parts of the completed work are put together. The plate, when inked and printed as a whole, ideally gives no clues to the piece-by-piece activity with which it was created.

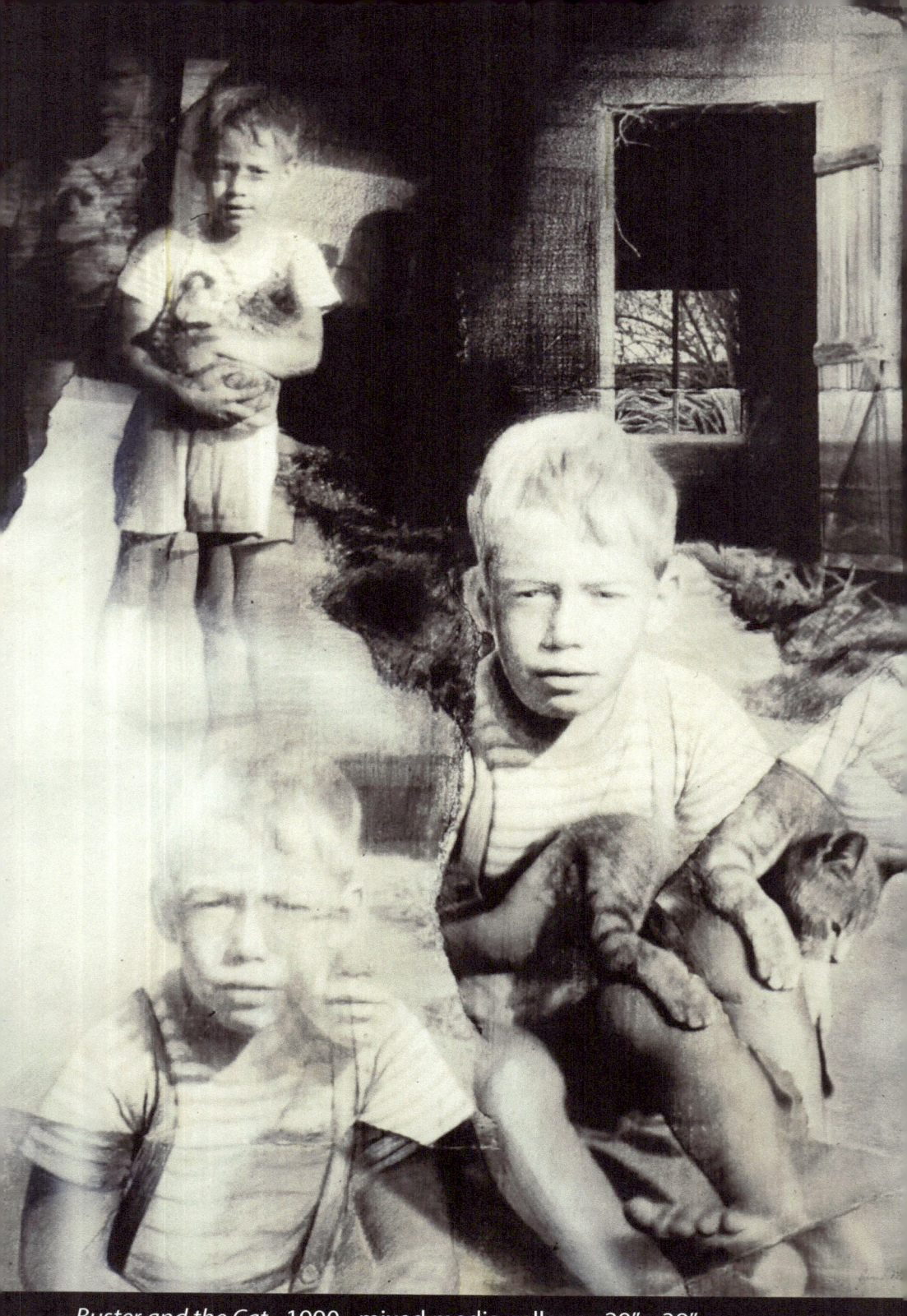

Buster and the Cat • 1990 • mixed media collage • 28" x 38"

The object of these works is not to try to make drawings look like photographs or to make photographs look like drawings, but to have a subtle blending of the two. A successful image will effectively use the best qualities of both drawing and photography. I have worked on incorporating photographically derived imagery into an imagined space to create a new context in which both exist simultaneously. I work with the photographic image because of its innate sense of believability, and I use intaglio as my medium because I believe the altering of a photographic image can be achieved better and more expressively on a tactile, physical surface as opposed to the flatness of photographic paper. Rosin aquatints are the intaglio counterpart to the silver grains in film, being variable by using either a finely applied box dusting or a grainier hand application of the rosin.

I experienced a technical breakthrough when switching from zinc to steel for my working surface. The original motivation for changing was the size limitation of the zinc available. I wanted my figures to be almost life size in my prints, similar to the collages I was working on, such as *Buster and the Cat.* While working with the steel I found the inherent grain of the steel and the way the acid worked

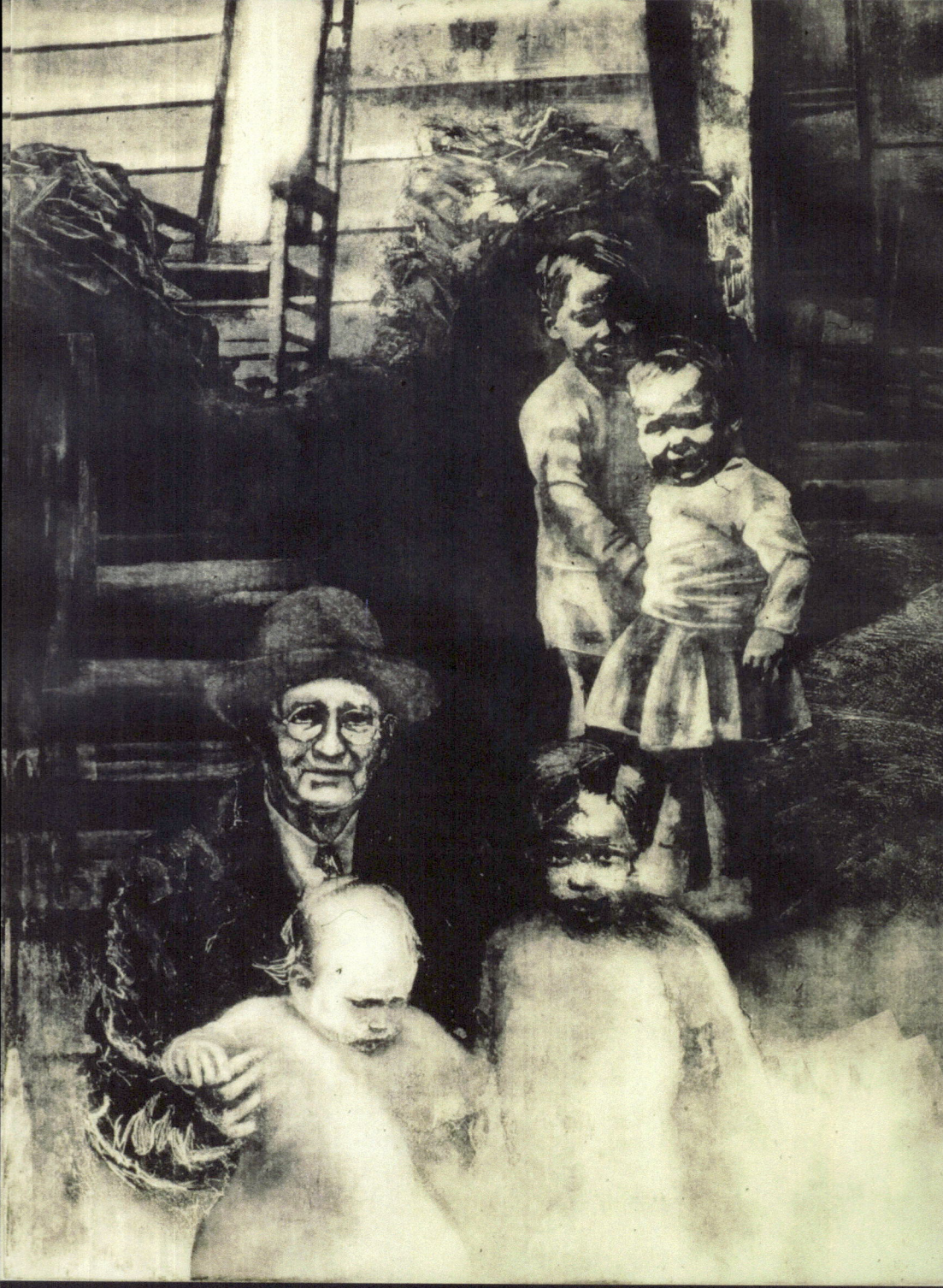
Wait—Don't Go • 1991 • intaglio • 36" x 48"

upon it was much more useful for my purposed than zinc, which has no grain. For example, I am able to obtain much more visiby expressive marks using a lithograph crayon and then etching the plate. The steel picks up every bit of grease put down and the acid bites accordingly and accurately. I used the lithograph crayon to enhance the figures on the first large steel intaglio, *Wait—Don't Go*. On this print I discovered its potential and have gradually taken it further, through *Portrait of My Uncle as a Cowboy* and then to *In Remembrance of the Porch Photos*. In *In Remembrance of the Porch Photos*, I began the piece with the drawing first and then added the photograph. I had previously begun my images with the photo first and then added the drawing to "correct" parts of the photo that had not developed well. The marking system of the lithograph crayon on steel was a liberation from the painstaking, finely detailed marking system of the etching needle which is physically fulfilling to use. My approach to the parts of each image has evolved from always having the figures presented in as "real" a fashion as possible, through using the photographic image. I am now questioning which parts of the image bear a closer connection with reality and believability, the photographic parts or the drawn parts. I

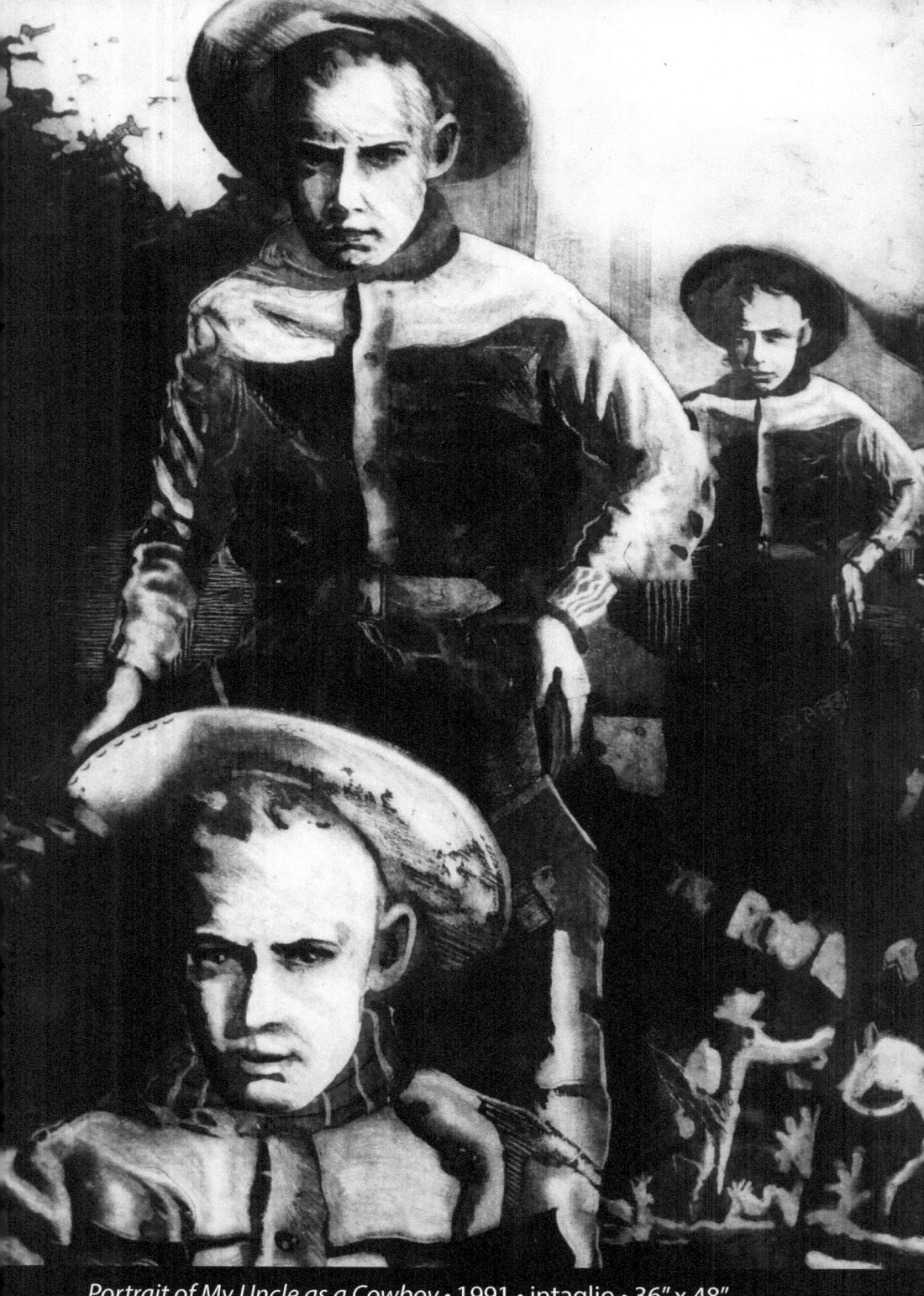
Portrait of My Uncle as a Cowboy • 1991 • intaglio • 36" x 48"

am trying to show that the two approaches can be equally believable when used in tandem.

My work contains images of figures to which I relate with a sense of nostalgia and familiarity. Most of the images in this body of work contain parts of old negatives shot by my relatives in the 1940s. In hundreds of negatives, my mother and my uncle are depicted as children, doing childish things. Looking at these photographs, I was struck by the similarity of them and photographs taken of my brother and me as children. I saw similarities in looks, manner, and poses. I chose to use these older negatives partly because they are larger and easier to work with than negatives made of my brother and me in the 1960s and 1970s. Also, I feel that using old negatives affords me the opportunity to acknowledge the traditions and gifts previous generations have made to my life as an artist. I have found that while pictures of children are often "loaded" images and cradled in sentimentality, they also encourage a basic level of understanding between generations. A common denominator between individuals is childhood, and regardless of what persona individuals choose to wear as an adult, they cannot escape the fact that they once were children. Using nostalgic

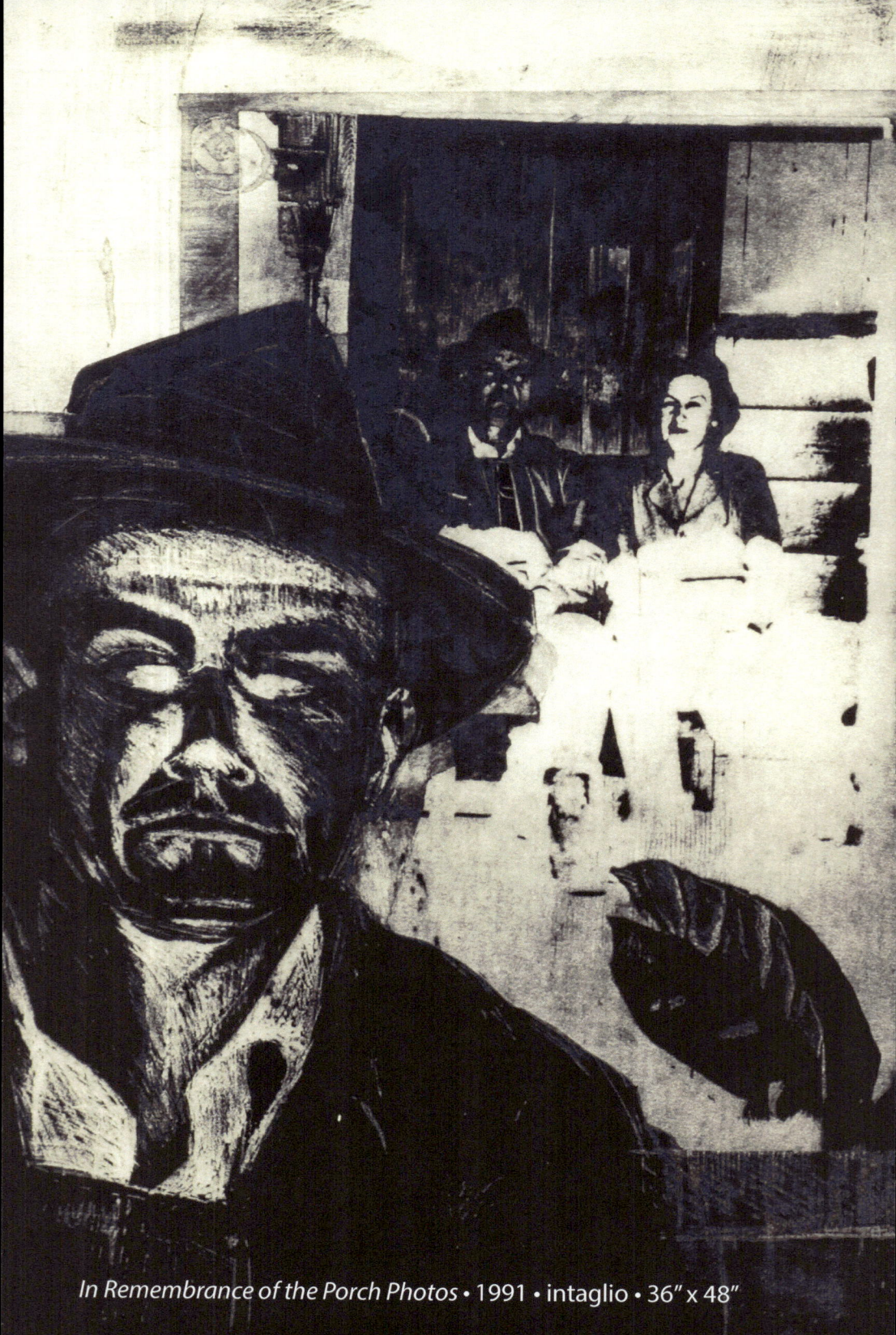

In Remembrance of the Porch Photos • 1991 • intaglio • 36" x 48"

images from the 1940s also evokes a feeling of innocence and makes a reference to an era I regard as a simpler time.

Of the negatives I have chosen to work with, I most appreciate those that were obviously shot in succession. Rarely was one photograph taken without another being shot immediately following it. Variations in poses and expressions lead to a timeless quality about the images, and I try to emphasize this quality in my intaglios and collages. The colleges, such as *Deluxe American Kitty Hostage,* approach the possibilities of combining drawing and photography in a much more visible manner than the intaglios. The collages deal with the photo/drawing issue more openly and honestly than the intaglios, because they are missing the step of being transferred to a plate and then printed in a cohesive format. I have attempted to make the most out of the edges and parts that are indications of the way I assemble a work. I have also had to take issue with the variety of warm and cool tones that come from using a variety of materials, such as prismacolor and spray paint. The photographic parts of the collages are done with the only commercially available photographic emulsion, *Liquid Light,* which is brushed onto Rives BFK paper.

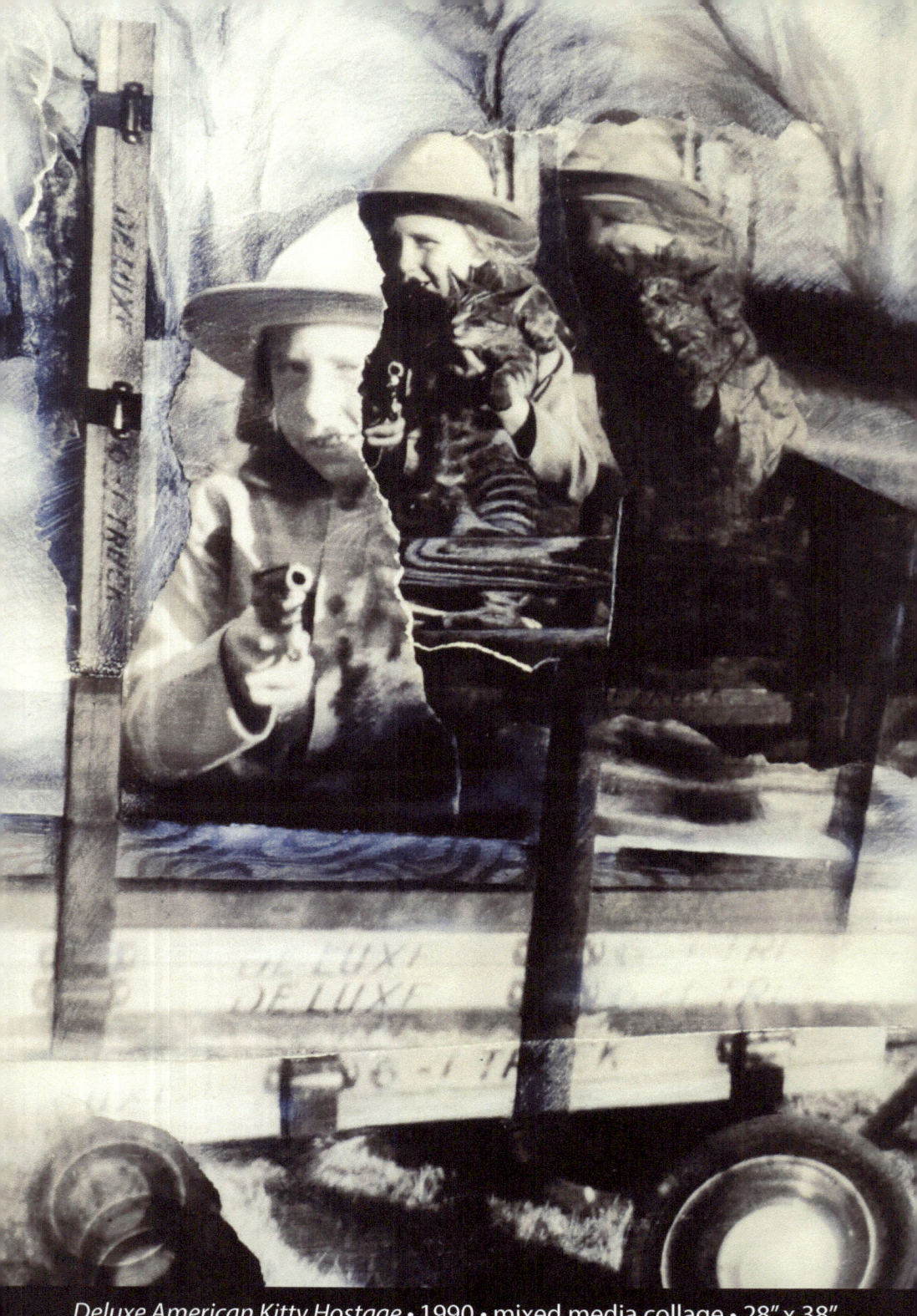

Deluxe American Kitty Hostage • 1990 • mixed media collage • 28" x 38"

Brushstrokes are left intentionally as a clue to the photograph/hand-applied mark problem I am addressing. While the emulsion parts of the piece contain a warm, greenish yellow cast, the drawing materials contrast with a cooler and more pure black and white. In these collages I also have the difference between drawn and photographic images indicated by a change in visual temperature.

I have indicated movement in both media by double exposing and double printing. Through the double exposure and double print approach, I would like to suggest what I believe to be the fundamental idea behind the family snapshot. Family snapshots remind me of the fact that people, things, and feelings exist for a second or a fraction of a second and then are gone. Time moves too fast to capture, even with a camera. Most of the negatives I am using were taken of everyday activities of children, such as the building of things. For example, in *Ideal Street Teepees,* the activity is not particularly noteworthy but it is the gesture of the child presenting her hand-made construction that makes the visual story worth telling. This image covers the timelessness and innocence I am trying to capture.

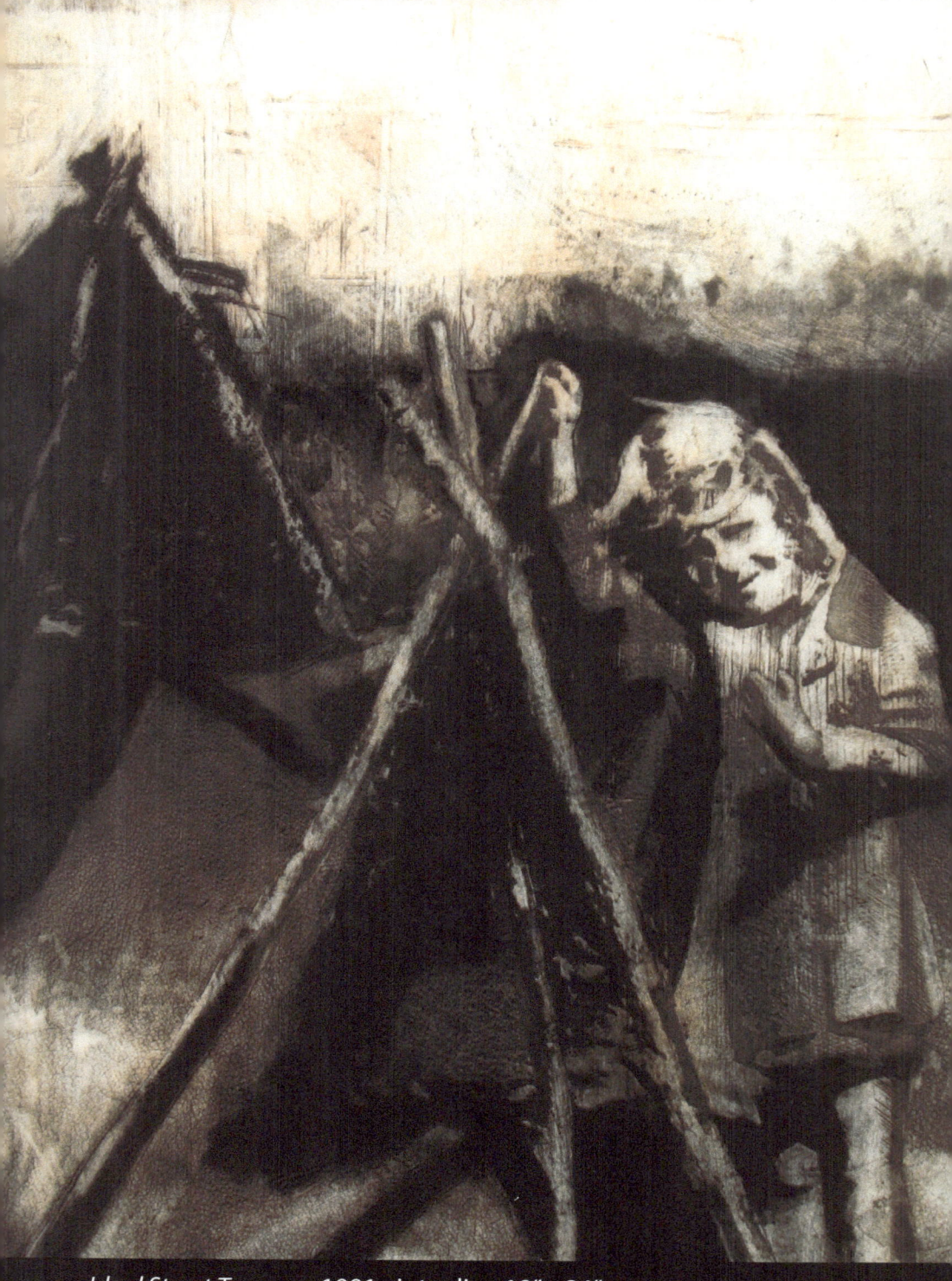

Ideal Street Teepees • 1991 • intaglio • 18" x 24"

Through my exploration evidenced in prints and collages I have worked toward a balance between the traditional and non-traditional means of image-making. My use of old family photographs pays homage to tradition and history, both my personal history and the history of photographic printmaking.

* * *

VITA

Ellen Elizabeth Moore was born in 1964 in Richmond, Virginia. In 1982 she entered East Carolina University in Greenville, North Carolina, and finished in December 1986. After traveling and working for a year, she entered the M.F.A. program at Louisiana State University in 1988 and finished in 1991.

M.F.A. Thesis Exhibition

April 20-26, 1991
Louisiana State University
Foster Hall Gallery, Baton Rouge
Opening Reception April 20, 7-9 PM

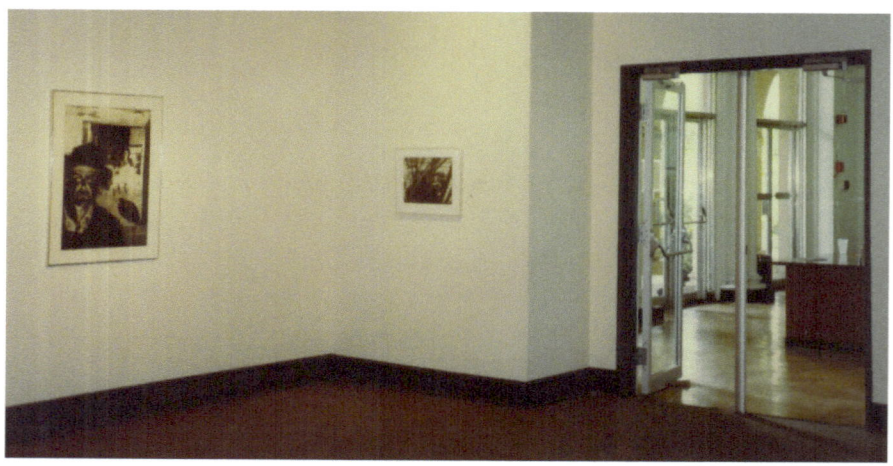

Entrance way to Foster Hall Gallery.
"In Remembrance of the Porch Photos" and "Ironworks"

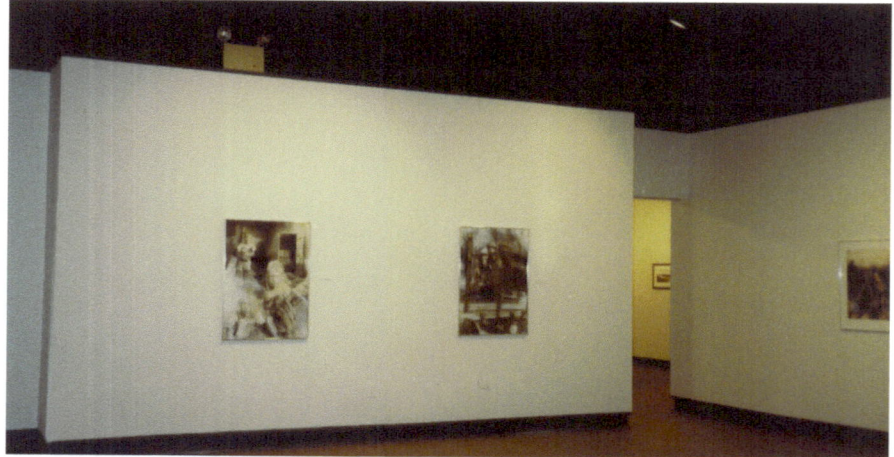

Main wall separating galleries.
"Buster and the Cat" and "Deluxe American Kitty Hostage."

addendum

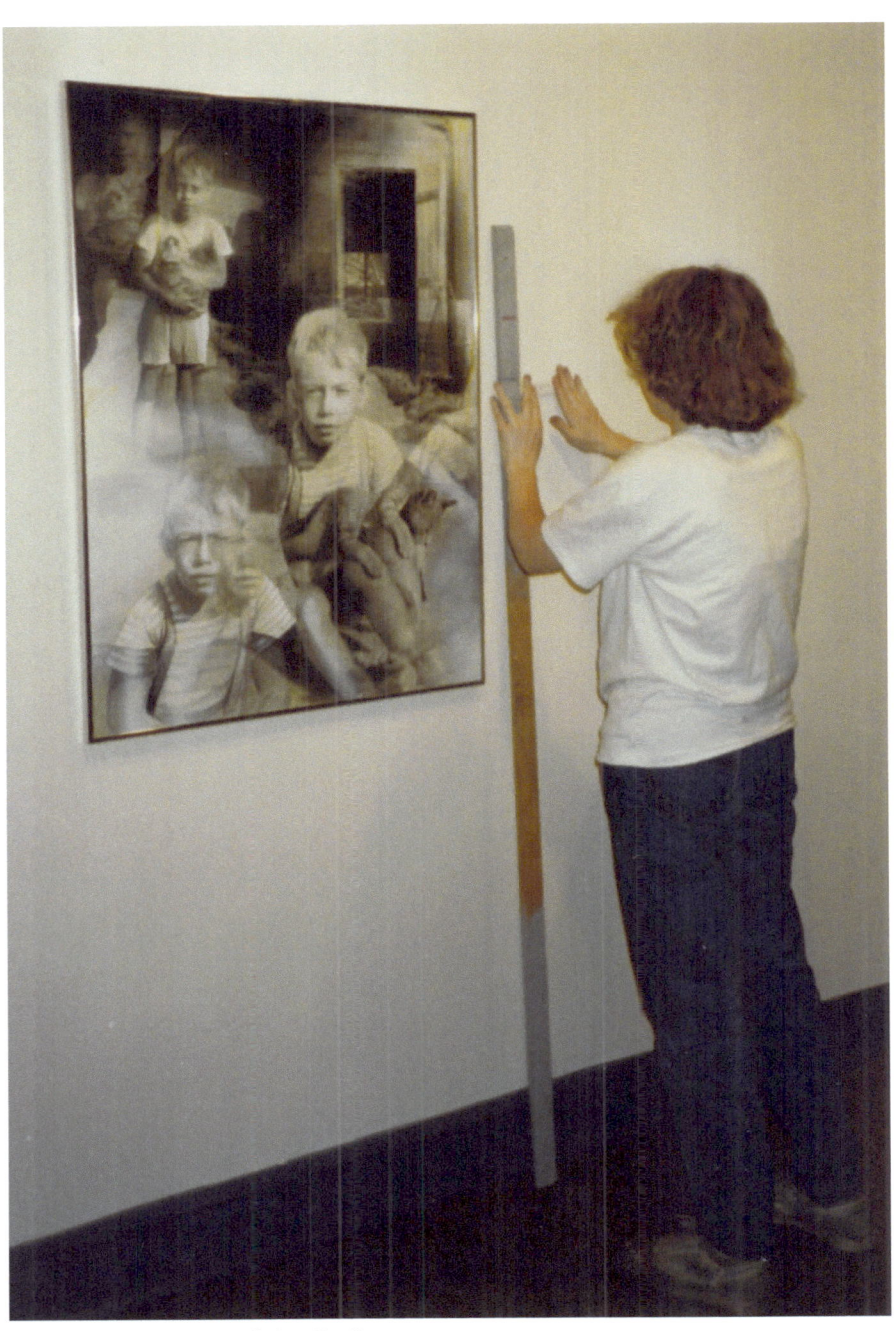

Hanging "Buster and the Cat."

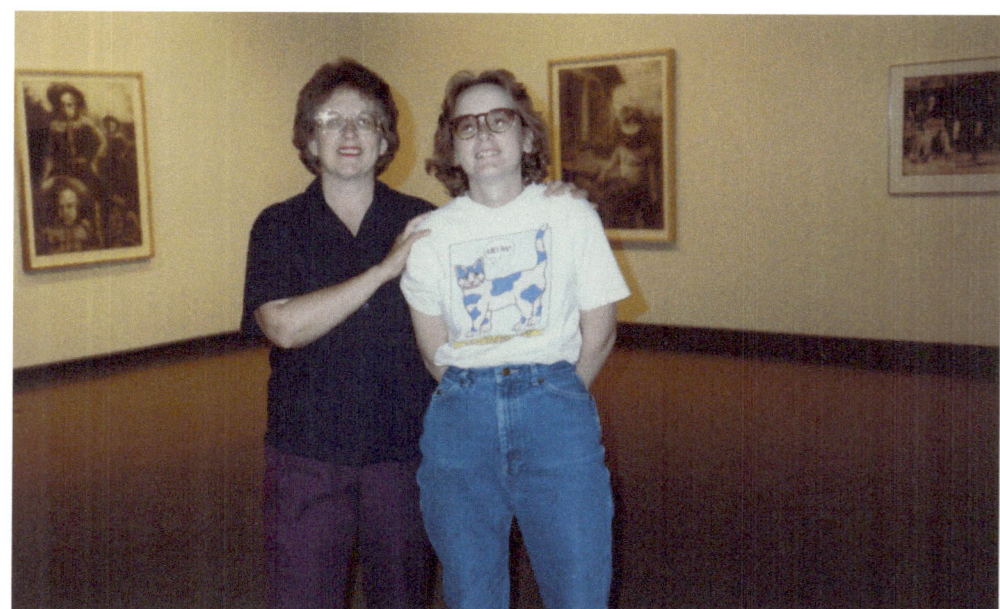

With Mom. Behind us is "Portrait of My Uncle as a Cowboy," another large intaglio "Untitled" featuring a boy and his dog, and "Porch Gathering."

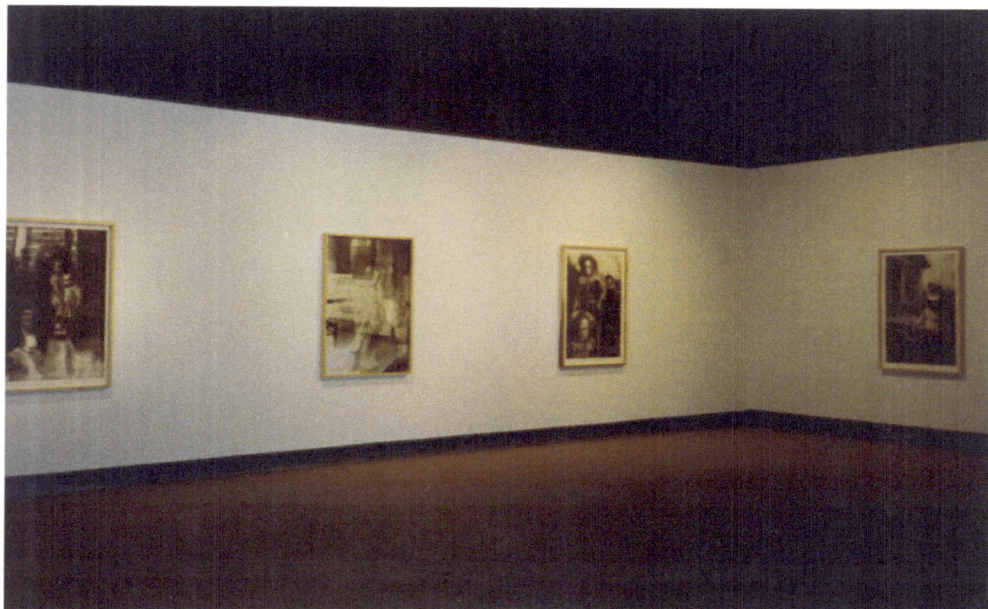

The largest pieces in the show were hung together. "Wait— Don't Go," "Boochie Boo Was Here," "Portrait of My Uncle as a Cowboy," and the "Untitled" intaglio all measured 3' x 4'.

addendum

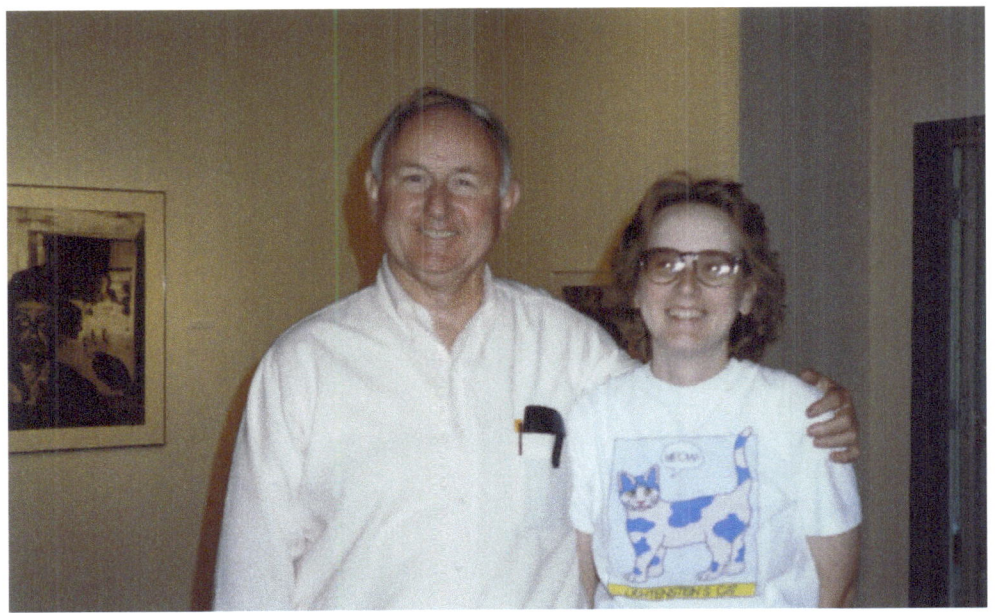

With Dad. Behind us is "In Remembrance of the Porch Photos."

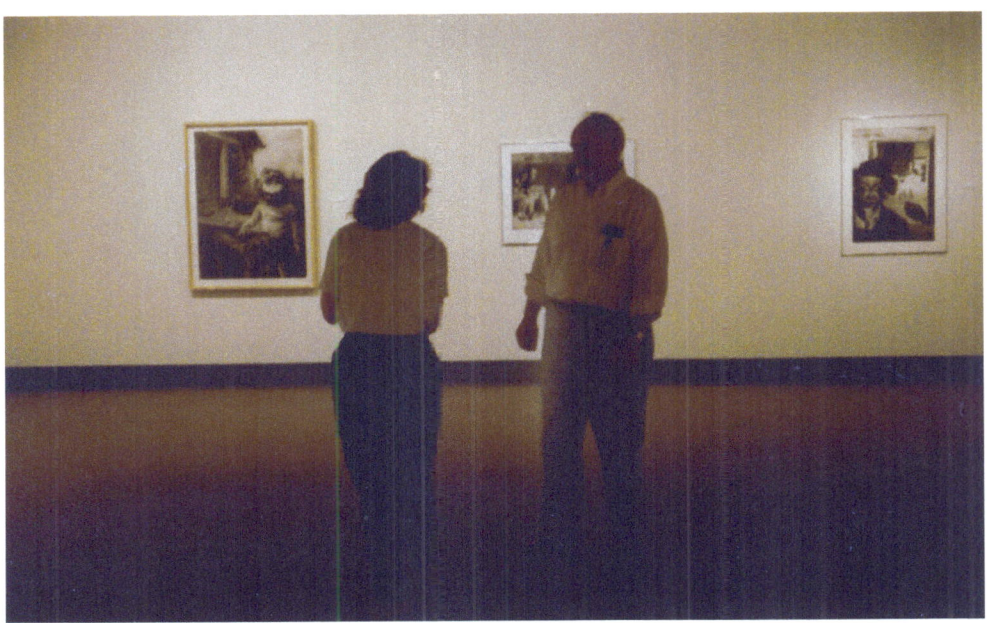

Sharing a laugh with Dad.

www.ingramcontent.com/pod-product-compliance
Lightning Source LLC
Chambersburg PA
CBHW040305220526
45473CB00002B/588